Don't Be a Donkey About Your Money:

A No-Nonsense Guide to Investment.

<u>Carol Sichembo writers,</u>

Introduction

- Why You Should Invest (Even If You Think It's Scary)
    - Building wealth for your future goals
    - Beating inflation and keeping your purchasing power
    - Achieving financial freedom
- Debunking Investing Myths
    - Investing is only for the rich
    - It's too complicated for beginners
    - You need a lot of money to get started

Part 1: The Donkey Investor and Why They Lose

- Chapter 1: The Fearful Donkey: Avoiding Analysis Paralysis
    - Information overload and decision fatigue
    - Fear of missing out (FOMO) vs. fear of losing out (FOOL)
    - Developing a rational investment strategy

- Chapter 2: The Greedy Donkey: Chasing Hot Tips and Short-Term Gains
    - The allure of get-rich-quick schemes
    - Recognizing and avoiding investment scams
    - Focusing on long-term wealth building
- Chapter 3: The Lazy Donkey: Why Procrastination Costs You Money
    - Overcoming the inertia to start investing
    - Setting achievable financial goals
    - The power of compound interest.

Part 2: The Savvy Investor: Building a Strong Financial Foundation

- Chapter 4: Understanding Your Risk Tolerance
    - Different risk profiles and investment styles
    - Assessing your comfort level with market fluctuations
    - Matching risk to your investment goals and timeline

- Chapter 5: Building Your Emergency Fund
    - The importance of a safety net
    - How much to save for emergencies
    - Choosing the right account for your emergency fund
- Chapter 6: Getting Your Debt Under Control
    - The burden of high-interest debt on investments
    - Strategies for paying down debt
    - Prioritizing debt repayment vs. investing

Part 3: Investing Basics for the Everyday Donkey

- Chapter 7: Asset Allocation and Diversification
    - Spreading your investments across different asset classes
    - Balancing risk and reward with diversification
    - Building a diversified portfolio
- Chapter 8: Understanding Common Investment Vehicles
    - Stocks, bonds, and mutual funds explained

- Exchange-Traded Funds (ETFs) - a low-cost option
- Choosing the right investments for your goals

- **Chapter 9: Dollar-Cost Averaging: Invest Like a Clock**
  - Reducing risk by investing regularly
  - Avoiding emotional investing and market timing
  - The benefits of consistency and discipline.

Part 4: Taking Action and Investing with Confidence

- **Chapter 10: Choosing the Right Investment Account**
  - Traditional IRAs and Roth IRAs for retirement savings
  - Brokerage accounts for managing your investments
  - Choosing a low-cost investment platform.

- **Chapter 12: The Wise Donkey Shares Timeless Investment Wisdom**

Conclusion

- Invest Smart, Not Hard: Recap of Key Points
- Taking Control of Your Financial Future: The Power of Starting Now
- Call to Action: Don't Be a Donkey - Start Investing Today!

Introduction: Don't Be a Donkey About Your Money!

Let's face it, investing can feel like a confusing maze filled with jargon, charts, and enough financial news to make your head spin. Maybe you've dabbled a toe in the water, only to lose interest or get scared by a market downturn. Perhaps you've been convinced by a "get rich quick" scheme that ended up leaving you feeling like a complete donkey.

Here's the good news: You're not alone. Millions of people feel the same way. But guess what? Investing doesn't have to be complicated, and it certainly shouldn't leave you feeling like a financial fool. This book is your guide to becoming a **Savvy Investor**, not a **Donkey Investor**.

We'll break down the basics in a clear, **no-nonsense** way, debunking myths and showing you how to build a strong financial foundation. You'll learn about different investment vehicles, how to manage risk, and develop a long-term strategy that works for you. Most importantly, we'll show you how to invest **smart and, not hard**.

Ready to ditch the fear and frustration? Let's get started on your journey to financial freedom! This book will equip you with the knowledge and confidence to **stop being a donkey about your money** and start building a brighter financial future. Buckle up, grab your metaphorical carrot, and get ready to invest like a pro!

Chapter 1: The Fearful Donkey: Taming the "Maybe Later" Monster

Let's be honest, diving into the world of investing can feel as daunting as staring down a mountain of paperwork on a Monday morning. Information overload hits you from all sides: complex charts, financial jargon that sounds like another language, and enough news articles to make your head spin. It's no wonder so many people end up feeling like a **Fearful Donkey**, paralyzed by indecision and that nagging voice in their head whispering, "Maybe later..."

Sound familiar? Maybe you're like Sarah, a fantastic teacher with a bright future, but the thought of picking stocks makes you break out in a cold sweat. Or perhaps you're David, a young entrepreneur with a great business idea, but the idea of deciphering stock charts makes you want to crawl back under the covers. Here's the truth: You're not alone. Millions of people feel the same way.

The problem is, this **analysis paralysis** can be a real wealth-killer. While you're busy overthinking every move, the market keeps chugging along, and potential opportunities pass you by. But fear not, fellow traveler! This chapter is your guide to taming the "Maybe Later" monster and taking control of your financial future.

We'll break down the biggest fears that keep people stuck on the sidelines and show you some simple strategies to overcome them. Here are some of the common anxieties we'll tackle:

- **Fear of Making the Wrong Choice:** Let's face it, nobody wants to lose money. But the good news is, investing isn't about picking the next overnight success story. It's about building a diversified portfolio for the long haul. Think of it like packing a suitcase for a trip – you wouldn't bring all your eggs in one basket, right? The same goes for investing. We'll show you how to spread your money across different assets to minimize risk.

- **Information Overload:** The financial world throws a lot of information at you, like a firehose of data. The key is to focus on reliable sources and learn to identify what's truly important. We'll give you some tips on finding trustworthy resources and separating the financial facts from the fiction.

- **Emotional Investing:** Our emotions can cloud our judgment, especially when it comes to money. We might panic and sell everything during a market downturn, or get swept up in the hype and chase hot stocks without a plan. We'll teach you how to keep your emotions in check and make sound investment decisions based on logic, not fear.

By the end of this chapter, you'll be equipped with the tools and knowledge to overcome your fear and take that first confident step towards a brighter financial future. Remember, investing is a marathon, not a sprint. So ditch the "Maybe Later" monster, grab your metaphorical saddle, and let's get started on this exciting journey together!

Chapter 2: The Greedy Donkey: Ditching the "Get Rich Quick" Mirage

Ah, the **Greedy Donkey**. We all know one (or maybe we've all been one at some point!). This donkey sees dollar signs everywhere, gets lured in by shiny promises of instant wealth, and ends up chasing "get rich quick" schemes that fizzle faster than a firecracker.

Remember Michael, your neighbor who quit his job to chase the latest cryptocurrency after reading a hyped-up online forum? Yeah, that's the Greedy Donkey in action. The truth is, there's no magic formula for overnight riches. Building wealth takes time, discipline, and a healthy dose of skepticism.

In this chapter, we'll expose the dangers of the Greedy Donkey mentality and show you how to become a **Savvy**

Investor who focuses on long-term growth, not fleeting gains. Here's what we'll cover:

- **The Allure of the "Get Rich Quick" Scheme:** Let's face it, the idea of effortless wealth is tempting. But here's the reality: most of these schemes are nothing more than a mirage in the financial desert, designed to separate you from your hard-earned cash. We'll unveil the red flags to watch out for and show you how to identify scams before they take a bite out of your savings.

- **The Power of Patience:** Building wealth is a slow and steady process, like watching a tree grow strong and tall. The Greedy Donkey craves instant gratification, but the Savvy Investor understands the power of patience and compound interest. We'll explain how even small investments, made consistently over time, can snowball into a significant nest egg.

- **Focus on Long-Term Goals:** The Greedy Donkey chases the next hot tip, but the Savvy Investor has a clear vision for the future. What are your financial goals? Retirement? A child's education? Once you know your goals, you can develop a long-term investment strategy that aligns with your needs and risk tolerance.

- **Developing a Disciplined Approach:** Investing requires discipline. The Savvy Investor sticks to their plan, avoids emotional knee-jerk reactions to market fluctuations, and doesn't get swayed by the latest fads. We'll provide tips on developing a disciplined investing routine and staying focused on your long-term objectives.

Real-life stories:

The Greedy Donkey Exposed:

- **Cryptocurrency Craze:** Remember the 2017-2018 boom and subsequent bust of the cryptocurrency market? Many people, just like Michael in your example, were lured in by the promise of massive returns and invested heavily in trendy cryptocurrencies based on online hype. Unfortunately, many lost a significant portion of their savings when the bubble burst. This is a classic example of the Greedy Donkey mentality leading to substantial losses.

The Savvy Investor Triumphs:

- **The Teacher Who Became a Millionaire:** Let's look at Amelia, a high school teacher who started investing small amounts of money consistently each month. Instead of chasing hot stocks, she focused on low-cost index funds and built a diversified portfolio over time. Through patience and discipline, Amelia was able to accumulate a significant nest egg, proving that slow and steady wins the race, even on a teacher's salary.

From Almost-Donkey to Savvy Investor:

- **David's Investment Journey:** David, the young entrepreneur from Chapter 1, initially felt overwhelmed by the investing world. However, after learning about the dangers of the Greedy Donkey mentality and the importance of a long-term strategy, he decided to educate himself. David started with small, regular investments in a diversified portfolio and focused on his long-term goals. By prioritizing education, patience, and discipline, David avoided the pitfalls of the Greedy Donkey and embarked on a successful investment journey.

Concise Takeaway:

- Building wealth is a marathon, not a sprint. Focus on long-term growth through a disciplined investment strategy, not fleeting gains from "get rich quick" schemes.

More Elaborate Takeaway:

- The allure of instant riches can be strong, but most "get rich quick" schemes are nothing more than mirages. Become a Savvy Investor by prioritizing education, developing a long-term plan, and focusing on patience and discipline in your investment approach. Remember, slow and steady wins the race!

Chapter 3: The Lazy Donkey: Why Putting Things Off Makes You Poorer (and How to Kick the Habit)

Let's face it, we all have a bit of the Lazy Donkey in us sometimes. That voice whispers, "Investing seems like a hassle," or "I'll start tomorrow," and suddenly, weeks or even months have flown by. But here's the thing: procrastination, the Lazy Donkey's best friend, can be a serious wealth-killer.

In this chapter, we'll explore the dangers of procrastination in investing and equip you with the tools to overcome this common hurdle. Here's what we'll cover:

- **The Cost of Delay:** Time is your greatest ally in investing. The earlier you start, the more time your money has to grow through compound interest. The Lazy Donkey who keeps putting things off misses out on this powerful tool. We'll show you with real-life examples how even a few years of delay can significantly impact your investment returns.

- **Overcoming Analysis Paralysis:** The Lazy Donkey might hide behind the excuse of "needing more information" to avoid taking action. While education is important, getting stuck in research mode can lead to paralysis. We'll provide tips on how to gather enough information to make informed decisions without getting overwhelmed.

- **Setting SMART Goals:** Vague goals like "get rich" aren't motivating. The Savvy Investor sets **SMART** goals (Specific, Measurable, Achievable, Relevant, and Time-bound). This clarity helps you develop a plan and take action. We'll walk you through the process of setting SMART financial goals that will keep you motivated and on track.

- **Developing Actionable Habits:** Building wealth requires consistent action. The Lazy Donkey might say, "I'll invest when I have more money," but the Savvy Investor starts small and invests regularly, even if it's just a little bit each month. We'll show you how to develop small, actionable habits that will make investing a breeze.

- **Automating Your Investments:** Technology is your friend! Many investment platforms allow you to set up automatic transfers, so you "set it and forget it." This removes the temptation to procrastinate and ensures your money is consistently working for you. We'll explain how to leverage automation to overcome the Lazy Donkey and stay on track with your investment goals.

The Cost of Delay:

- **Lisa: The Missed Opportunity:** Lisa, a young professional, always thought about investing but kept putting it off, thinking she needed more money to "get started properly." Ten years later, she realized she'd missed out on a decade of potential growth due to procrastination. Even small, regular investments over those ten years could have compounded significantly, leaving her in a much better financial position.

Overcoming Analysis Paralysis:

- **Mark: From Research Rabbit Hole to Savvy Investor:** Mark spent months researching every possible investment option, becoming overwhelmed by the sheer amount of information. Finally, he realized this analysis paralysis was preventing him from taking action. He focused on learning the basics, chose a diversified portfolio, and started investing, vowing to continue learning alongside his journey.

Setting SMART Goals:

- **Sarah: From Vague Dreams to Concrete Plan:** Sarah used to dream of "being financially secure someday." However, this vague goal lacked direction. She transformed into a Savvy Investor by setting a SMART goal – save 10% of her salary each month towards a retirement fund within the next five years. This clear, actionable goal motivated her to start investing and track her progress.

Developing Actionable Habits:

- **David (from Chapter 2): Small Steps, Big Results:** Remember David, the entrepreneur who overcame the Greedy Donkey mentality? He also battled the Lazy Donkey initially. However, he started small by setting up an automatic transfer of $50 every week into his investment account. This small, consistent action helped him overcome procrastination and build a solid investment foundation.

Chapter 4: Understanding Your Risk Tolerance: Don't Be a Daredevil or a Scaredy-Cat in Investing

Imagine yourself on a roller coaster. Some folks love the heart-pounding drops and twists, while others prefer a tamer ride. Investing is kind of similar. There's a certain level of risk involved, and how comfortable you are with that risk is your **risk tolerance**.

This chapter is all about understanding your risk tolerance, which is basically your personal comfort level with potential ups and downs in the investment world. We won't use fancy financial jargon here, just a clear breakdown to help you figure out what kind of investor you are.

Risk and Reward: Two Sides of the Coin

Think of risk and reward as two sides of the same coin. Investments that have the potential for higher returns (think big profits!) also tend to carry a higher risk of losing money (yikes!). On the other hand, investments with lower risk typically offer lower returns (slower and steadier growth).

The Risk Tolerance Spectrum

Here's a spectrum to visualize different risk tolerances:

- **The Daredevil Investor:** These folks crave excitement and are comfortable with significant ups and downs. They might invest in things like high-growth stocks or emerging markets, aiming for big returns but accepting the possibility of big losses.
- **The Moderate Investor:** This is the "Goldilocks zone" for many people. Moderate investors are comfortable with some risk, aiming for a balance between growth and stability. They might invest in a mix of stocks, bonds, and other assets.
- **The Conservative Investor:** These folks prioritize safety and security. They're comfortable with lower potential returns in exchange for less risk. They might

invest in things like bonds, certificates of deposit (CDs), or money market accounts.

So, How Do You Know Where You Fit In?

Here are some questions to ask yourself:

- **How would you react to a sudden drop in your investment value?** Would you panic or stay calm?
- **What's your time horizon?** Are you saving for retirement in 20 years, or a down payment on a house in 2 years? The longer your time horizon, the more risk you might be able to tolerate.
- **What are your financial goals?** Are you aiming for aggressive wealth accumulation or just building a safety net?

By answering these questions, you can get a better sense of your risk tolerance. Remember, there's no right or wrong answer – it's all about finding what feels comfortable for YOU.

The Savvy Investor's Tip: Don't be afraid to seek professional advice from a financial advisor who can help you assess your risk tolerance and develop an investment strategy based on your individual needs and goals.

In the next chapter, we'll dive deeper into building a strong financial foundation, no matter your risk tolerance!

Chapter 5: Building Your Emergency Fund: Your Financial Safety Net

Imagine this: your car sputters to a stop, the washing machine overflows, or an unexpected medical bill lands in your mailbox. These emergencies can wreak havoc on your finances, but having a solid **emergency fund** can be your saving grace.

Think of your emergency fund as a financial safety net, a pool of money set aside specifically for unexpected expenses. It's not about getting rich quick, but about having peace of mind knowing you can handle life's little curveballs without going into debt or dipping into your long-term investments.

Why is an Emergency Fund Important?

Here's why building an emergency fund is a crucial step for any Savvy Investor:

- **Peace of Mind:** Knowing you have a financial cushion reduces stress and allows you to focus on resolving the emergency, not panicking about the cost.
- **Avoid Debt:** Unexpected expenses can easily derail your financial goals if you have to rely on credit cards or high-interest loans. An emergency fund helps you avoid debt and its associated charges.
- **Protect Your Investments:** Having to sell your investments to cover an emergency can disrupt your long-term financial plans. An emergency fund ensures your investments stay on track for future goals like retirement.

How Much Should You Save?

A good rule of thumb is to aim for an emergency fund that covers 3-6 months of your living expenses. This can vary depending on your circumstances. If you have a stable job and good health insurance, you might be comfortable with a smaller fund. However, if you're self-employed or have a high-risk job, you might need a larger buffer.

Getting Started with Your Emergency Fund:

Here are some tips to jumpstart your emergency fund:

- **Set a SMART Goal:** Decide how much you want to save and set a realistic timeframe. Break it down into smaller, achievable goals. For example, aim to save $200 per week for 6 months.
- **Automate Your Savings:** Set up automatic transfers from your checking account to your emergency fund savings account. This "set it and forget it" approach ensures consistent saving.
- **Find Extra Cash:** Look for ways to cut expenses or generate extra income through side hustles or selling unused items. Every little bit adds up!

Choosing the Right Account for Your Emergency Fund:

- **High Liquidity:** Your emergency fund needs to be easily accessible. Choose an account that allows you to withdraw your money quickly without penalties.
- **Low Risk:** Don't invest your emergency fund in risky assets that could lose value. Consider a high-yield savings account or a money market account.

Building your emergency fund is a crucial step towards financial freedom. It provides peace of mind, helps you avoid debt, and protects your long-term investments. Start small, be consistent, and watch your safety net grow!

Imagine this: Sarah, a hardworking single mom, wakes up to a flooded basement. The panic sets in – the repairs will be expensive, and her paycheck isn't due for another two weeks. But Sarah isn't fazed. She pulls out her emergency fund, a financial safety net she's been diligently building, and breathes a sigh of relief. The flood may have caused a mess, but thanks to her emergency fund, Sarah can handle the repairs without going into debt or jeopardizing her bills.

This is the power of an emergency fund. It's not about getting rich quick, but about having peace of mind knowing you can weather life's unexpected storms, big or small.

How Much Should You Save?

A common target is 3-6 months of your living expenses. This can vary depending on your situation. David, a freelancer with a variable income, aims for a larger emergency fund (closer to 6 months) to account for potential income fluctuations. On the other hand, Maria, a teacher with a stable job and good health insurance, feels comfortable with a smaller fund (around 3 months).

Financial stress can definitely strain relationships with family and coworkers. Here are some ways to address it:

- **Financial Independence and Self-Reliance:** Frame building wealth as a way to achieve financial independence and reduce reliance on others. This allows you to handle emergencies without burdening loved ones and gives you more control over your life.
- **Open Communication:** Discuss the importance of open communication with family and friends. Maybe you need to explain your financial goals to your partner or discuss childcare options with family if you're considering a side hustle.
- **Healthy Boundaries:** Financial stress can lead to resentment. Talk about setting healthy boundaries with family, like politely declining unsolicited financial

advice or impulse purchases that don't align with your budget.

- **The Power of "No":** practice saying "no" to requests you can't afford, whether it's a loan from a coworker or a lavish vacation with friends. A responsible "no" protects your financial future and strengthens relationships in the long run.
- **Focus on Solutions:** Instead of dwelling on the fear of being a burden, focus on solutions. The book itself is a tool to help readers achieve financial security and avoid relying on others.

Chapter 6: Getting Your Debt Under Control.

Forget the damsel in distress! In this chapter, you're the hero on a quest to slay a fearsome beast: the Debt Dragon. This fire-breathing monster loves to hoard your hard-earned cash, leaving you feeling trapped and powerless. But fear not, brave investor! With the right tools and unwavering determination, you can conquer this financial foe and emerge victorious.

Debt can be a heavy burden, weighing you down and stealing your financial freedom. Maybe you're drowning in credit card bills, student loans are a constant source of stress, or that car loan feels like a never-ending chain around your ankle. Whatever your debt dragon looks like, it's time to grab your metaphorical sword (aka a **debt-slaying strategy**) and take back control!

Why Tackle Debt Now?

Here's why slaying the Debt Dragon is crucial for every aspiring Savvy Investor:

- **Free Up Your Cash Flow:** Debt payments eat away at your hard-earned money, leaving less for saving and investing towards your dreams. Conquering debt frees up cash for you to invest in your future, not someone else's bottom line.
- **Improve Your Credit Score:** High debt and missed payments can damage your credit score. A good credit score unlocks better interest rates on loans, mortgages, and even insurance. Slaying the Debt Dragon paves the way for a healthier financial future.
- **Gain Peace of Mind:** Debt can be a constant source of stress and anxiety. By taking control and developing a plan to eliminate it, you'll gain peace of mind and unlock a sense of financial empowerment.

Strategies for Debt Slaying:

There's no one-size-fits-all approach, but here are some powerful weapons in your debt-slaying arsenal:

- **The Debt Avalanche:** Focus on paying off the debt with the highest interest rate first, regardless of the balance. This saves you money in the long run.
- **The Debt Snowball:** Focus on paying off the smallest debt first, regardless of interest rate. Seeing quick wins can boost your motivation and keep you on track.
- **Budgeting Like a Boss:** Create a budget that tracks your income and expenses. Identify areas where you can cut back and free up resources to put towards debt payments.
- **Boost Your Income:** Consider a side hustle, a raise negotiation, or selling unused items to generate extra income to accelerate your debt payoff.

Remember, you're not alone in this fight! There are amazing resources available online and through financial advisors to help you develop a personalized debt-slaying strategy. Don't be afraid to seek out support and guidance.

The Road to Financial Freedom

Conquering the Debt Dragon is an epic journey, but the rewards are worth it. Imagine a future where you're not chained to debt payments. Imagine a future where you have more control over your finances and the freedom to pursue your goals. This is the power of becoming a Savvy Investor.

So, grab your metaphorical sword (and maybe a budgeting app!), and let's slay that Debt Dragon together! Remember, every debt payment is a victory, every dollar saved is a step closer to financial freedom. The path to wealth starts with taking control of your finances, and slaying the Debt Dragon is the first step on this exciting adventure!

Meet Michael, the Monster Tamer:

Michael, a young entrepreneur, found himself drowning in student loans after graduating. The Debt Dragon had him feeling overwhelmed and discouraged. But Michael refused to give up. He researched different debt repayment strategies, ultimately choosing the Debt Avalanche method to tackle his high-interest loans first. He also created a strict budget, cutting back on unnecessary expenses like eating out and subscriptions he never used. Finally, Michael took on a side hustle as a freelance writer to generate extra income for faster debt payments. It wasn't easy, but with dedication and perseverance, Michael slayed the Debt Dragon! He paid off his student loans in just three years, a testament to his courage and commitment.

Introducing Sarah, the Snowball Slayer:

Sarah, a single mom, found herself struggling with credit card debt accumulated over the years. The monster's constant demands for minimum payments felt like a never-ending cycle. Sarah learned about the Debt Snowball method and decided to focus on paying off the smallest debt first, regardless of interest rate. Seeing those smaller debts disappear quickly gave her a much-needed boost of motivation. She also started budgeting every penny, utilizing free budgeting apps to track her spending and identify areas to cut back. Sarah's journey wasn't a sprint, but a steady march towards financial freedom. Every paid-off credit card statement felt like a victory, and after two years of focused effort, Sarah finally slayed the Debt Dragon!.

Chapter 7: Asset Allocation and Diversification: Building a Balanced Investment Portfolio

Imagine a delicious pie. A good investment portfolio is like that pie – a combination of different ingredients (assets) working together to create something wonderful (financial growth). But just like a pie wouldn't be very tasty with all sugar, a successful investment portfolio needs balance. This chapter dives into **asset allocation** and **diversification**, the cornerstones of building a balanced and resilient portfolio.

Asset Allocation: The Big Picture

Think of asset allocation as the recipe for your investment pie. It's the process of dividing your investment dollars among different asset classes based on your risk tolerance, investment goals, and time horizon. Here's a breakdown of some common asset classes:

- **Stocks:** Represent ownership in companies. They offer the potential for high returns, but also come with higher risk of price fluctuations.
- **Bonds:** Represent loans you make to companies or governments. They offer lower risk and typically lower returns compared to stocks.
- **Cash Equivalents:** Highly liquid assets like savings accounts or money market accounts. They offer minimal risk and minimal returns.
- **Real Estate:** Can be directly owned or invested in through Real Estate Investment Trusts (REITs). Offers diversification and potential for long-term growth, but comes with its own set of risks like property management or vacancy periods.

The Importance of Diversification

Diversification is the secret ingredient in your investment pie. It's the concept of spreading your money across different asset classes to reduce overall risk. Think of it like not putting all your eggs in one basket. If one asset class performs poorly, the others can help balance it out.

Here's an analogy to illustrate diversification:

- **Investing in One Stock:** Imagine you invest all your money in a single tech company. If that company's stock price plummets, your entire portfolio takes a hit.
- **Diversified Portfolio:** Now, imagine you spread your investment across different sectors – tech, healthcare, consumer staples. If the tech sector goes through a downturn, the other sectors might still be performing well, minimizing the overall impact on your portfolio.

Finding Your Asset Allocation Sweet Spot

There's no one-size-fits-all approach to asset allocation. The ideal mix of assets for you depends on several factors:

- **Risk Tolerance:** Are you comfortable with potential ups and downs in the market, or do you prefer a more conservative approach?
- **Investment Goals:** Are you saving for retirement in 20 years, or a down payment on a house in 5 years? Your time horizon influences your risk tolerance.
- **Age:** Generally, younger investors can tolerate more risk as they have a longer time horizon for their investments to recover from market fluctuations.

Here's a simplified example:

- **Aggressive Investor:** This investor might have a higher percentage of their portfolio in stocks (seeking higher returns) with a smaller allocation to bonds and cash equivalents (lower risk, lower returns).
- **Moderate Investor:** This investor might have a balanced portfolio with a mix of stocks, bonds, and cash equivalents.
- **Conservative Investor:** This investor might focus on lower-risk assets like bonds and cash equivalents, with a smaller allocation to stocks.

Rebalancing Your Portfolio

The market is constantly changing. As your investments grow (or shrink) over time, your asset allocation can get out of whack. **Rebalancing** involves periodically adjusting your portfolio to maintain your target asset allocation. This may involve buying or selling certain assets to ensure your risk profile remains aligned with your goals.

Building a Balanced Investment Portfolio

By understanding asset allocation and diversification, you can take control of your financial future. Here are some tips for building a balanced portfolio:

- **Assess Your Risk Tolerance:** Be honest with yourself about how comfortable you are with market fluctuations.

- **Define Your Investment Goals:** Knowing what you're saving for helps determine your time horizon and risk tolerance.
- **Research Different Asset Classes:** Educate yourself about the pros and cons of different asset classes.
- **Consider a Target Date Fund:** These pre-made portfolios adjust their asset allocation automatically as you approach your target retirement date.
- **Seek Professional Guidance:** Financial advisors can help you create a personalized investment plan based on your unique circumstances.

The Donkey and the Diversification Dilemma: Why Spreading Your Eggs is Crucial

Remember our friend, the Donkey, from earlier chapters? Well, he's back, and this time, he's facing a new challenge: investing. Unfortunately, the Donkey hasn't quite shaken off his old habits.

The Donkey's Risky Recipe:

Imagine the Donkey, ever the gambler, decides to invest all his money in the stock of a hot new tech company. He's convinced it's the next big thing, a surefire path to riches. This is a classic example of the **Donkey Putting All His Eggs in One Basket**. While the potential for high returns is tempting, it's also incredibly risky. If the tech company's stock price plummets (and let's face it, even the hottest companies can go bust), the Donkey loses everything. His investment pie is a disaster – all sugar and no substance, offering no stability or protection against potential downturns.

The Savvy Investor's Balanced Pie:

The Savvy Investor, on the other hand, approaches investing with a more balanced and diversified approach. They understand the importance of **spreading their eggs across different baskets**.

The Takeaway:

Remember, the Savvy Investor doesn't put all their eggs in one basket. By embracing diversification, you can build a balanced and resilient investment portfolio that helps you weather market storms and achieve your financial dreams. So, ditch the Donkey's risky recipe and embrace diversification for a sweeter investment future!

Chapter 8: Investment Vehicles for the Savvy Investor: Beyond Donkey Baskets

Now that you understand the importance of diversification, it's time to explore the different vehicles you can use to build your investment portfolio. Think of these vehicles as the baskets you'll use to hold your investment eggs (remember the Donkey's one-basket mistake?). Each vehicle offers unique advantages and caters to different investment goals. Let's dive in!

Mutual Funds and ETFs:

- Imagine a basket prefilled with a variety of stocks or bonds. Mutual funds and Exchange-Traded Funds (ETFs) are like that. They pool money from many investors and invest it in a diversified mix of assets, following a specific investment strategy.
- **Mutual Funds:** Professionally managed funds that offer a variety of investment options, from broad market exposure to sector-specific investing. The

Donkey, even the delegator, might choose a mutual fund to avoid picking individual stocks.

- **ETFs:** Similar to mutual funds but trade on stock exchanges throughout the day like individual stocks. The Savvy Investor might choose a low-cost ETF for its transparency and tax efficiency.

Individual Stocks:

- For the hands-on investor, individual stocks offer the potential for higher returns (and higher risks) by investing directly in companies you believe in. The Donkey, still yearning for excitement, might be tempted to chase "hot stocks" – a risky strategy for the faint of heart.
- **The Savvy Investor's Approach:** Thorough research is key! They carefully analyze companies' financials, understand the industry, and only invest in companies with strong fundamentals and long-term growth potential.

Bonds:

- Think of bonds as IOUs from governments or corporations. You invest money, and they pay you interest over a set period, returning your principal at maturity. Bonds offer stability and income, but typically lower returns than stocks.
- **The Donkey, always looking for a quick buck, might scoff at bonds.** But the Savvy Investor understands their role in diversification and uses them to balance their portfolio and generate predictable income.

Real Estate:

- Investing in real estate can be a great way to build wealth and generate passive income through rental payments. However, it requires significant upfront capital and ongoing management responsibilities.

- **The Donkey might see real estate as a "get rich quick" scheme.** But the Savvy Investor understands it's a long-term investment requiring research, due diligence, and potentially professional property management.

There are many other investment vehicles available, and the best choices for you will depend on your risk tolerance, investment goals, and time horizon. Here are some additional tips:

- **Do your research!** Educate yourself about different investment options before putting your money in anything.
- **Start small and diversify!** Don't jump in headfirst. Start with a small investment and gradually build your portfolio with a variety of vehicles.
- **Consider professional advice!** A financial advisor can help you create a personalized investment plan based on your unique circumstances.

Dodging Donkey Disasters: Avoiding Pyramid Schemes and Other Investment Traps.

Our friend the Donkey is back, and this time, he's stumbled upon a flyer promising "get rich quick" schemes. Uh oh, the Donkey's susceptibility to easy money traps is a recipe for disaster! Let's help him avoid these pitfalls and steer him towards smart investment strategies.

The Pyramid Scheme Pitfall:

The flyer Donkey found is advertising a "revolutionary new product" with an "unbelievable income opportunity." It sounds too good to be true, because it probably is. This is a classic sign of a **pyramid scheme**. These schemes focus on recruiting new members to pay fees, rather than selling actual products or services. The money from new recruits flows up the pyramid, enriching those at the top, while leaving those at the bottom with nothing but empty pockets.

Here's why Donkey should avoid pyramid schemes like the plague:

- **Unsustainable Model:** Pyramid schemes rely on continuous recruitment, which is mathematically impossible to maintain. Eventually, the well runs dry, and the scheme collapses, leaving many at the bottom with financial losses.

- **Focus on Recruitment, Not Products:** Legitimate businesses focus on selling quality products or services. Pyramid schemes prioritize recruiting new members to generate income, often with little to no regard for the actual product's value.

- **Exorbitant Fees:** Pyramid schemes often charge high upfront costs or require participants to purchase overpriced products. This can be a significant financial burden for those involved.

The Savvy Investor's Guide to Avoiding Scams:

So, how can Donkey (and you!) avoid falling prey to pyramid schemes and other investment traps? Here are some golden rules:

- **If it Sounds Too Good to Be True, It Probably Is:** Extraordinary returns with little to no risk are a red flag. Legitimate investments require research, effort, and a degree of risk tolerance.
- **Do Your Research:** Before investing in anything, research the company, the product, and the opportunity thoroughly. Read reviews, check with financial regulators, and don't be afraid to walk away if something feels off.
- **Beware of Pressure Tactics:** Legitimate investment opportunities won't pressure you into a quick decision.

If someone is rushing you to invest or making promises that seem too good to be true, walk away.

- **Seek Professional Advice:** If you're unsure about an investment opportunity, consider consulting a registered financial advisor. They can help you assess the risks and potential rewards involved.

Donkey, Remember: There's no shortcut to building wealth. Focus on smart, long-term investments and avoid get-rich-quick schemes. By educating yourself and making informed decisions, you can become a Savvy Investor and achieve your financial goals.

The next chapter will explore how to manage your emotions and make sound investment decisions, even when the market gets shaky.

Chapter 9: Dollar-Cost Averaging: Invest Like a Clock - Building Wealth Rain or Shine

Imagine this: you're determined to build a sandcastle masterpiece on the beach. But the tide keeps changing - sometimes calm and gentle, other times crashing in fierce waves. Building a successful investment portfolio can feel similar. The market has its ups and downs, but just like the tide eventually recedes, so too will market downturns.

This chapter introduces a powerful strategy called **Dollar-Cost Averaging (DCA)**, your secret weapon for building wealth consistently, regardless of market fluctuations.

The DCA Advantage:

Think of DCA as your automatic sandcastle-building tool. Here's how it works:

- **Invest Regularly:** Instead of investing a lump sum, you commit to investing a fixed amount of money at regular intervals (weekly, monthly, etc.)
- **Embrace the Long Haul:** DCA is a long-term strategy. By consistently investing, you purchase more shares when prices are low and fewer shares when prices are high.
- **Reduce Risk:** DCA helps you avoid the temptation of "timing the market" (an impossible feat!). By consistently buying, you average out the cost per share over time, mitigating the impact of market volatility.

DCA in Action: A Tale of Two Investors

Let's meet Michael, the Market Timer (who doesn't actually exist!), and Sarah, the DCA Devotee. Both have $100 to invest every month for a year. The stock price fluctuates throughout the year (imagine the rising and falling tide).

- **Michael, the Market Timer:** He tries to time the market, investing his entire $100 when he thinks the price is low and holding off when he thinks it's high. Unfortunately, market timing is notoriously difficult, and Michael ends up buying at various price points throughout the year.

- **Sarah, the DCA Devotee:** Unfazed by market fluctuations, Sarah faithfully invests her $100 every month, regardless of the price. This consistent approach averages out her cost per share over time.

The Result? At the end of the year, Sarah, the DCA Devotee, might hold more shares than Michael, the Market Timer, simply by investing consistently.

The Power of Consistency:

DCA isn't about getting rich quick. It's about building wealth steadily and strategically, like a magnificent sandcastle that withstands the tide. Here's why DCA is a masterpiece in the making:

- **Reduces Emotional Investing:** DCA removes the temptation to panic-sell during downturns or over-invest during market highs. It keeps your emotions in check and promotes a disciplined approach.
- **Accessibility for Everyone:** DCA allows you to start investing with smaller amounts, making it a great strategy for beginners or those with limited capital.
- **Long-Term Focus:** DCA encourages a long-term investment mindset, which is crucial for building wealth and achieving your financial goals.

DCA: Your Investment Clock

Think of DCA as your investment clock. Set a regular investment schedule and stick to it, just like clockwork. Over time, your consistent investments will accumulate, like grains of sand building a magnificent sandcastle. Remember, even the most impressive sandcastles start with a single grain of sand, and consistent investment, even in small amounts, can lead to a substantial portfolio over time.

Yes, business ownership can be considered a form of investment. In fact, it can be a very lucrative one, offering the potential for high returns. However, it's important to remember that business ownership also carries significant risks. Here's a breakdown of the pros and cons to consider:

Pros:

- **High Potential Returns:** Successful businesses can generate significant profits for the owner.
- **Equity and Control:** Business owners have control over the direction and operations of their company.
- **Personal Satisfaction:** Building and running a successful business can be very rewarding.

Cons:

- **High Risk:** Many businesses fail, especially in the early stages. Owners may lose their entire investment.
- **Time Commitment:** Running a business requires a significant amount of time and effort.
- **Stressful:** Business ownership can be very stressful, especially when facing financial challenges.

Focus Beyond Stocks and Bonds:

While stocks and bonds are traditional investment options, there's a whole world of possibilities beyond them. Here are some additional investment vehicles to consider:

- **Real Estate:** Investing in rental properties can provide passive income and long-term capital appreciation.
- **REITs (Real Estate Investment Trusts):** Invest in real estate without the hassle of property management.
- **Peer-to-Peer Lending:** Loan money directly to individuals or businesses and earn interest on your investment.
- **Commodities:** Invest in raw materials like gold, oil, or wheat, but be aware of the price fluctuations.

- **Cryptocurrency (Risky):** A relatively new and volatile asset class with the potential for high returns (and high losses).

Remember:

- **Diversification is Key:** Don't put all your eggs in one basket. Spread your investments across different asset classes to manage risk.
- **Do Your Research:** Before investing in anything, understand the risks and potential rewards involved.
- **Consider Professional Advice:** A financial advisor can help you create a personalized investment plan based on your unique circumstances and risk tolerance.

By exploring different investment options beyond just stocks and bonds, you can build a diversified portfolio that aligns with your financial goals. Business ownership can be a powerful path to wealth creation, but remember to carefully weigh the risks and rewards before taking the plunge.

Chapter 10: Choosing the Right Investment Account: Your Investment Home

Congratulations! You've embraced smart investing strategies like DCA and are ready to pick your investment vehicle (remember, that's your basket for holding investments). But before you jump in, you need a suitable home for those investments – an **investment account**. Think of it as your personal investment sanctuary.

This chapter dives into the different types of investment accounts available and helps you choose the one that best suits your goals.

The Account All-Stars:

Here are the main contenders in the investment account arena:

- **Taxable Brokerage Accounts:** These accounts offer a wide range of investment options, including stocks, bonds, ETFs, and more. There are no restrictions on contributions or withdrawals, but you'll pay taxes on any capital gains (profits from selling investments). This account is ideal for long-term investment goals or for actively managing your portfolio.
- **Retirement Accounts:** These accounts offer tax advantages to encourage saving for retirement. Popular options include:
    - **Traditional IRAs:** Contributions may be tax-deductible (reducing your taxable income), and earnings grow tax-deferred until withdrawal in retirement (usually at age 59 ½), when they are taxed as income.

- **Roth IRAs:** Contributions are made with after-tax dollars (not deductible from your current income), but **earnings grow tax-free** and qualified withdrawals in retirement are also tax-free. There are contribution limits for both IRAs.
- **Employer-Sponsored Retirement Accounts:** Many employers offer retirement plans like 401(k)s. These accounts allow you to contribute pre-tax dollars directly from your paycheck, reducing your taxable income. Earnings grow tax-deferred until withdrawal in retirement, which are then taxed as income. Some employers even match a portion of your contributions, essentially giving you free money!

Choosing Your Champion:

The right account for you depends on your investment goals, time horizon, and tax situation. Here's a quick guide:

- **For Long-Term Growth (Taxable or Retirement):** If you're saving for a distant goal like retirement, a taxable brokerage account or a retirement account (traditional IRA, Roth IRA, or employer-sponsored plan) could be a good fit. Consider the tax implications and contribution limits of each option.
- **For Short-Term Savings (Taxable):** If you're saving for a closer goal like a down payment on a house, a taxable brokerage account might be suitable. You'll have easy access to your funds, but remember to pay taxes on capital gains.

Additional Account Options:

- **Health Savings Accounts (HSAs):** These accounts allow you to save for qualified medical expenses with tax-deductible contributions, tax-free growth, and tax-free qualified withdrawals.
- **Coverdell Education Savings Accounts (ESAs):** Contribute to a child's education with tax advantages, though there are restrictions on withdrawals.

Remember:

- **Consider your goals:** Are you saving for retirement, a down payment, or a short-term need? Choose an account that aligns with your timeline.
- **Think about taxes:** Taxable accounts offer flexibility but come with tax implications. Retirement accounts offer tax benefits but have contribution limits and withdrawal rules.
- **Seek professional advice:** A financial advisor can help you navigate the different account options and choose the one that best suits your unique circumstances.

With the right investment account in place, you're ready to start building your investment portfolio and taking control of your financial future.

The Donkey's back, and this time, his distrust of banks is rearing its head again. He's hesitant to open an investment account because, well, banks. But fear not, Donkey! There are plenty of safe and secure options for your hard-earned money, even for those wary of traditional banks. Let's explore some alternatives:

Understanding Investment Custodians:

Investment accounts aren't always held by banks. **Investment custodians** specialize in holding your investments for safekeeping, similar to a safety deposit box for your stocks, bonds, and other assets. These custodians are regulated by financial authorities, ensuring your investments are protected. Unlike banks, custodians typically don't offer loans or checking accounts, focusing solely on safeguarding your investments.

Donkey-Friendly Account Options:

Here are some investment account options that might appeal to the security-conscious Donkey:

- **Online Brokerage Firms:** Many online brokers offer investment accounts with robust security features and a wide range of investment options. They often have lower fees compared to traditional banks. Research the firm's reputation and security measures before investing.
- **Robo-advisors:** These automated investment platforms offer a low-cost, hands-off approach. They invest your money according to your risk tolerance and goals, using a custodian to hold your assets securely.
- **Direct Stock Purchase Plans (DRIPs):** Some companies allow you to invest directly in their stock, bypassing traditional brokerage firms. While offering limited investment options, DRIPs can be a good fit for Donkey if he wants to invest in a specific company he trusts.

Security Matters Most:

No matter which account option you choose, prioritize security. Here's what to look for:

- **Two-factor Authentication:** This adds an extra layer of security by requiring a code from your phone or email in addition to your password when logging in.
- **Encryption:** Look for an account provider that uses strong encryption to protect your personal information.
- **Regulation:** Ensure the custodian or brokerage firm is regulated by a reputable financial authority.

The Savvy Donkey Takes Charge:

Donkey doesn't have to rely solely on banks for his investment journey. By exploring alternative custodian accounts and prioritizing security features, he can find a safe and secure haven for his investments.

Chapter 12: The Wise Donkey Shares Timeless Investment Wisdom

The wise Donkey, with a patient gaze and a gentle bray, offers timeless investment wisdom gleaned from the fields of finance and the proverbs of old. Heed his words, dear reader, and navigate the investment landscape with both prudence and prosperity.

The Virtue of Patience: A Seed Takes Time to Sprout

The wise Donkey reminds us, "A single grain does not fill a barn, nor a single day bring riches." Just as a farmer sows seeds and waits for the harvest, so too must the investor plant their capital and exercise patience. Building wealth is a gradual process, not a race to instant riches.

Diversification: A Hedge Against the Whims of Wind

The wise Donkey observes, "A wise donkey walks not on a single path, lest a sudden storm leave him stranded." Diversification, the spreading of investments across various asset classes, is a cornerstone of sound investing. Just as a sturdy fence protects a field from unpredictable winds, diversification protects your portfolio from market fluctuations.

Beware the Siren Song of Greed: A Donkey Chasing Two Carrots Loses Both

The wise Donkey warns, "The allure of quick gains can blind even the most discerning eye." Be wary of promises of exorbitant returns, for they often mask excessive risk. Focus on long-term growth and avoid chasing fleeting trends or get-rich-quick schemes.

Knowledge is Power: A Donkey Who Reads Scrolls is Wiser Than One Who Grazes Alone

The wise Donkey advises, "Seek knowledge before venturing into the market's vast pastures." Educate yourself on investment principles, asset classes, and risk management. Read books, consult with financial advisors, and continuously expand your understanding of the financial world.

Know Your Limits: A Donkey Does Not Attempt to Pull a Cart Meant for an Ox

The wise Donkey cautions, "Invest according to your means and risk tolerance." Don't be tempted to overextend yourself in pursuit of unrealistic returns. Understand your risk tolerance and invest accordingly, ensuring a comfortable night's rest even when the market churns.

Emotions are Fickle Beasts: A Donkey Led by His Ears Walks in Circles

The wise Donkey emphasizes, "Let not fear or excitement guide your investment decisions." The market's ups and downs can trigger emotional reactions. Stick to your long-term strategy and avoid impulsive decisions driven by fear or greed.

Time is Your Ally: A Seedling Slowly Becomes a Mighty Oak

The wise Donkey reminds us, "The power of time and compound interest is a force to be harnessed." Start investing early and let your money grow over time. The earlier you begin, the more time your investments have to compound and flourish.

The Market is a Fickle Creature: A Donkey Does Not Predict the Weather

The wise Donkey acknowledges, "The market's movements are like the wind, ever-changing and difficult to predict." Don't waste your energy trying to time the market. Focus on a long-term strategy and remain disciplined through market fluctuations.

Seek Guidance When Needed: A Donkey Lost on the Path Asks for Direction

The wise Donkey encourages, "There is no shame in seeking help from those who have walked the path before." Consult with a qualified financial advisor for personalized guidance tailored to your unique circumstances. A trusted advisor can help you navigate the complexities of the market and make informed investment decisions.

Remember, dear reader, the wise Donkey's words are like seeds of wisdom. Sow them in your fertile mind, nurture them with knowledge and discipline, and watch your financial future blossom with prosperity.

Conclusion.

The wise Donkey, with a final thoughtful bray, reminds us that the journey to financial security is not a solitary one. The fields of investment may seem vast and ever-changing, but with knowledge, discipline, and a touch of diversification, anyone can build a path to prosperity. So, take a page from the Donkey's book – embrace continuous learning, manage your emotions, and don't be afraid to explore new investment horizons. Remember, the most valuable asset you possess is your financial education. Invest in yourself, invest wisely, and watch your future flourish like a field of golden grain, ripe for the harvest.